CW01660090

DO I KNOW MY BELOVED

PROPHET MUHAMMAD ﷺ?

A SIMPLIFIED DESCRIPTION
FROM THE SHAMĀ'IL OF THE BELOVED PROPHET ﷺ
FOR TEENAGERS & BEGINNERS

MOHAMMED AHMED

Published By

The FCPM
Fan Club of the Prophet
of Mankind ﷺ

Leicester, England

www.thefcpm.com
fcpm@hotmail.co.uk

White Fountain Publishing Ltd.

Leicester, England

www.whitefountain.co.uk
admin@whitefountain.co.uk

How Well Do I Know My Beloved Prophet?
Mohammed Ahmed

ISBN	978-1-7399907-4-9
Typesetting & Book Design	M.A. – White Fountain Publishing Ltd.
Cover Design	M.A.

CONTENTS

بِسْمِ ٱللَّهِ ٱلرَّحْمَٰنِ ٱلرَّحِيمِ

INTRODUCTION

Allah says in the Qur'ān:

﴿ لَقَدْ كَانَ لَكُمْ فِي رَسُولِ اللَّهِ أُسْوَةٌ حَسَنَةٌ ﴾

"*Indeed, in the Messenger of Allah, you have a beautiful example to follow.*" [Qur'an 33:21]

The Prophet Muḥammad (ﷺ) was sent by Allah as a mercy to humanity; rather a mercy to the universe. His life exemplifies how we should behave in all aspects of our lives—whether in our relationships, our work, our worship, our character, and all aspects of our lives. He was and will remain the best example of a human being, embodying humility, kindness, honesty, and patience.

But how well do we truly know him? Do we know about his character, his habits, his appearance, and how he lived his life? This booklet is an attempt to help you understand your beloved Prophet (ﷺ) more deeply. By knowing him, we can begin to follow in his footsteps and bring his beautiful character into our own lives.

Who Should Be Our Role Model?

It is in our very nature as humans to imitate. Since infancy, we begin to observe, perceiving what those around us do, and then we adopt selected behaviour. For decades psychologists have debated why we copy others. Irrespective of the various theories presented, it is common knowledge that human imitates.

Often, role models are adopted. Someone who leads or has led an exemplary life that we admire and feel we can emulate easily becomes the object of admiration. An ideal role model, due to their greatness, presents us with the opportunity to follow and imitate and reap something of that greatness ourselves.

As teenagers, it's common to look up to celebrities, athletes, or influencers. One may admire their success, their talents, or their beauty. But have you ever wondered why? Is it because of their fame, or because they genuinely have good character? Do they set a positive example for us to follow?

While many people in the world may have talents or beauty, no one is more worthy of our admiration and love than the last and final Prophet and Messenger Muḥammad (ﷺ). Loving our Beloved Prophet (ﷺ) is from the essential elements of our faith.

Anas (رضي الله عنه) reports, 'A Bedouin once asked the Messenger of Allah (ﷺ) when Judgement Day was.

"*What have you prepared for it?*" asked the Prophet (ﷺ).

"Not much in the way of great prayers and (extra) fasts," replied the Bedouin, "but I do love Allah and his Messenger (ﷺ)."

The Messenger of Allah (ﷺ) replied "*A man will be with whom he loves.*"

Anas (رضي الله عنه) adds, 'The Muslims did not rejoice at anything after the gift of Islam as they did at hearing these words!' (Reported by Tirmidhī and Ibn Ḥibbān).

He didn't seek fame or wealth; instead, he lived a life of service, humility, and compassion.

His greatness wasn't in material success, but in his closeness to Allah and the love he showed to others.

مُحمّدٌ بشرٌ ليسَ كالبشرِ   الياقوتُ حجرٌ ليسَ كالحجرِ

Muḥammad (ﷺ) is a human but not like other humans,
A ruby is a stone, but not like other stones.

Allah Himself chose him to be the guide for all of humanity.

The Prophet Muḥammad (ﷺ) once said: "*I leave you two things which, if you hold fast unto, you will not go astray: the Book of Allah and my way.*"

By following his example, we can strive to succeed not just in this world, but Allah willing, it will also guarantee our success in the Hereafter.

The more you know about a person,
the more you can prove to love them.

Sīrah* and *Shamā'il

When studying the life of the Prophet Muhammad (ﷺ), it's important to understand that there are two parts to learning about him:

(1) ***Sīrah*** (biography): which covers the major events of his life—his birth, prophethood, struggles, and victories.
(2) **Shamā'il** (features/characteristics): which focuses on the personal details of his life, such as his appearance, habits, and personality traits.

While the *Sīrah* gives us a historical understanding of the Prophet's (ﷺ) life, the *Shamā'il* helps us get to know him on a deeper, more personal level.

By learning about his gentle character, how he looked, and how he treated people, we can begin to connect with him not just as a Prophet, but also on a personal level with which we can relate to and love even more.

The study of *Shamā'il* helps us feel closer to the Prophet (ﷺ) as a person and inspires us to follow his beautiful example in our own lives.

This Booklet

This booklet is a summary of *Shamā'il*, specially designed for teenagers and beginners, but also for all lovers of our beloved (ﷺ), to help us discover and fall further in love with him in a simple and relatable way.

It is hoped that through this booklet, we can together embark on a journey to not only deepen our understanding and love for our beloved Prophet Muḥammad (ﷺ), but also to achieve the spiritual goals of emulating his noble character, adopting his *Sunnah*, and committing ourselves to his mission.

We pray that through this, we may be able to nurture a lasting spiritual connection with our beloved Prophet (ﷺ), be blessed with a drink from his refreshing white fountain of *al-Kawthar* on the Day of Judgment, and enjoy his eternal companionship in Jannah, *Āmīn.*

May eternal salutations, peace, and blessings be upon our beloved Prophet Muhammad (ﷺ), his noble family, and all his companions, forever and always.

Mohammed Ahmed

Night of Jumu 'ah
9 Rabī al-Awwal 1446 A.H.

www.thefcpm.com

WHAT DID MY BELOVED PROPHET (ﷺ) LOOK LIKE?

The companions of the Prophet (ﷺ) loved him deeply and described his appearance in detail. Their descriptions reveal not only his outer beauty but also the inner beauty that radiated from him.

Umm Ma'bad (رضي الله عنها) described the appearance of the Prophet (ﷺ) by saying that she saw a man whose beauty was luring, and whose face was so luminous that it dazzled the eyes. Alongside his apparent beauty, all inner virtues were embodied in him.

- **Height:** The Prophet (ﷺ) was of medium height, not too tall and not too short, with broad shoulders that gave him a strong and dignified appearance.

- **Hair:** The Prophet's (ﷺ) hair was long, slightly wavy and often reached his earlobes or above his shoulders, falling onto his blessed neck. He frequently oiled and combed his hair every other day to keep it neat, commencing from the right side.

At times, the Prophet (ﷺ) would part his hair, while at other times he would leave it unparted, allowing it to fall naturally.

It is also reported that he occasionally arranged his hair into four curls, reflecting his simple yet graceful appearance.

Qatādah once asked Anas ibn Mālik (رضي الله عنه) how the Prophet's (ﷺ) hair looked, and he replied, "*It was not very straight nor was it very curly; it came to rest between his ears and shoulders.*" (Reported by Bukhārī)

- **Beard:** The Prophet (ﷺ) had a full, black beard. He would comb and perfume it frequently. He commanded his followers to let their beards grow. At the time of his passing away, he had no more than twenty white hairs in his blessed beard.

- **Eyes:** His eyes were large and dark, with long lashes, giving them a striking yet gentle appearance. Jābir ibn Samurah (رضي الله عنه) described the Prophet's (ﷺ) eyes as having slight redness in the whites, adding to their distinctiveness.

His eyebrows were arched, thin, long and full, but not bushy. They were close to each other but not joined together.

- **Smile:** The Prophet (ﷺ) smiled often, and his smile was radiant. It is said that when he smiled, his teeth shone like pearls and light emitted from the gap between his teeth.

His smile made people feel loved and welcomed. 'Abdullāh ibn Mughīrah (رضي الله عنه) narrated, "*I never saw the Prophet except that he was smiling.*" (Reported by Al-Ḥākim).

The companions who saw the Prophet (ﷺ) were often struck by his beauty, inside and out. Barrā' ibn 'Āzib (رضي الله عنه) remarked, "*I have never seen anything more beautiful than the Prophet (ﷺ) wearing a red cloak.*" (Reported by Bukhārī).

The Ḥadīth of 'Alī ibn Abī Ṭālib (ﷺ)

When 'Alī (ﷺ) would describe the Prophet (ﷺ), he would say:

- *'He was not very tall nor short, but of* ***medium stature*** *among people.*
- *His* ***hair*** *was neither very curly nor very straight, but had a* ***slight wave*** *in it.*
- *He was not fat nor was his* ***face*** *fully rounded. It was however* ***slightly rounded****. The* ***complexion*** *was* ***white with redness*** *in it. His* ***eyes (irises)*** *were the* ***blackest*** *of all and* ***eyelashes*** *the* ***longest****.*
- *His* ***skeletal joints*** *were* ***large*** *and the area between his* ***shoulders*** *was* ***prominent****.*
- *He was scarce in* ***bodily hair****, but had a thin line of it running down the centre of his chest.*
- *His* ***palms*** *and* ***feet*** *were* ***fleshy****.*
- *When he* ***walked****, he lifted his legs forcefully, as if he were* ***descending*** *to a downward slope.*
- *When he addressed somebody, he turned his whole body towards the person.*

- *The* ***seal of prophethood*** *was situated (on his back) between his shoulder blades. He was the last of all Prophets.*
- *He was the most* ***generous*** *and* ***truthful*** *of all people.*
- *He was the most* ***tender*** *in* ***temperament*** *and came from the most noble of families.*
- *Any person who saw him suddenly would become* ***overawed****, and one who met him with recognition would* ***love*** *him.*
- *One describing him would say,* **'I have never seen a person like him, neither before nor after him** (ﷺ).'

(Reported by Tirmidhī).

The Prophet Muḥammad's (ﷺ) complexion was described as bright and glowing, ***fair with a rosy tint***, with a slight reddish hue, and a ***balanced tone***, which added to the aura of his presence, described by many Companions as more dazzling than the full moon.

- **Sa'd ibn Jarīr** (رضي الله عنه) reported, "The Prophet (ﷺ) had a white *complexion*, which was **slightly reddish**." (Reported by Muslim).

- **Anas ibn Mālik** (رضي الله عنه) noted that the Prophet's (ﷺ) *complexion* was neither extremely white nor very dark, but a **balanced and radiant hue**. Anas said, "The Prophet (ﷺ) was neither very tall nor very short. His complexion was neither very white nor very dark. His hair was neither straight nor curly, but it was wavy."

- **'Alī** (رضي الله عنه) described: "The Prophet (ﷺ) was not too tall, nor was he too short. His hair was slightly wavy, his *complexion* was **white with a**

reddish tint, and his eyes were the blackest of all. His palms were soft and his joints were large."

- **Jābir ibn Samurah** (رضي الله عنه) reported: "The Prophet (ﷺ) had a wide mouth, and there were red lines in the whiteness of his eyes. He had little flesh on his heels."

- **'Ā'ishah** (رضي الله عنها) narrated: "The Prophet's (ﷺ) hair was between ear length and shoulder length. His beard was full, and he used to frequently oil his hair and beard."

His luminous complexion, along with his radiant smile, made his presence striking and comforting to those around him.

Poem of Ḥassān ibn Thābit (رضي الله عنه):

Ḥassān ibn Thābit (رضي الله عنه), a renowned poet, was among the fortunate Companions blessed with the honor of praising the Prophet Muhammad (ﷺ) through his eloquent poetry.

In the presence of the Prophet (ﷺ), Ḥassān (رضي الله عنه) would compose and recite verses that celebrated the Prophet's noble character and unmatched beauty, using his poetic talents to defend and elevate the honour of the Prophet (ﷺ) and the message of Islam. One of his famous poems he recited was:

وَأَحْسَنُ مِنْكَ لَمْ تَرَ قَطُّ عَيْنٌ
وَأَجْمَلُ مِنْكَ لَمْ تَلِدِ النِّسَاءُ
خُلِقْتَ مُبَرَّءً مِنْ كُلِّ عَيْبٍ
كَأَنَّكَ قَدْ خُلِقْتَ كَمَا تَشَاءُ

Eyes have never seen anyone more beautiful than you,
No woman has ever given birth to one more handsome.
You were created free from every flaw,
As if you were created just as you wished.

The Prophet Muḥammad (ﷺ) wore clothing that was simple, modest, and practical. His garments reflected his humility, yet they were elegant, clean and dignified.

His dress usually consisted of a sheet wrap (*ridā'*) and a lower waist-wrap garment (*izār*) – i.e. similar to *iḥrām* worn in *Ḥajj/'Umrah* – made of coarse cloth. He is also reported to have worn woollen clothing.

He would wear whatever was available and was not at all bothered about what type of cloth it was made from or what design it was. As long as it covered the body and was modest, the Prophet (ﷺ) would not be against wearing it.

- **Upper Garment (*Qamīṣ*):** The Prophet (ﷺ) often wore a long shirt, known as a *qamīṣ*. Umm Salamah (رضي الله عنها) reported, "*The most beloved item of clothing to the Prophet (ﷺ) was the long shirt.*"

The *qamīṣ* was loose, covering his body comfortably without being restrictive.

His buttons would at times be left unfastened.

His sleeves reached past his wrists.

- **Lower Garment (*Izār*):** He also wore a lower garment, known as an *izār*, which was a simple wraparound cloth tied at the waist. It usually reached mid-shin or ankle length.

Salamah ibn Al-Aqwaʿ (رضي الله عنه) described how the Prophet's lower garment would sit, saying, "This is how my companion's (the Prophet's) lower garment was." (Reported by Tirmidhī)

- **Turban (ʿ*Imāmah*):** The Prophet (ﷺ) frequently wore a turban, which was common among the Arabs. Jābir ibn ʿAbdullah (رضي الله عنهما) narrated that when the Prophet ﷺ entered Makkah, he was wearing a **black turban**.

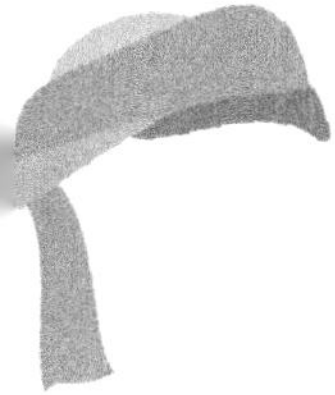

His Companions also noted that when he wore a turban, the tails of the turban sometimes hung down his back between his shoulders.

- **Colours:** The Prophet (ﷺ) encouraged wearing **white** clothing, saying, "*Wear white, for it is pure and clean, and shroud your dead in it.*" (Reported by Al-Ḥākim).

He also wore **red-striped garments** from Yemen, which made him appear particularly radiant.

He also wore **dark** garments and **sandy-coloured** clothing. On some occasions, he wore **green** garments, which are also often associated with paradise, as in the Holy Qur'ān. He also wore **black** coloured clothing.

He forbade males from wearing gold, silk, pure reddish colours as well as yellowish clothing.

- **Simplicity and Practicality**: The Prophet (ﷺ) wasn't concerned with fashion or luxury. He wore whatever was available to him, whether it was cotton, wool, or even simple cloth from

Yemen. As long as his clothes were modest and functional, he was content.

- **Garments from Yemen & Byzantine**: Anas ibn Mālik (ﷺ) reported that one of the Prophet's (ﷺ) favourite garments were from Yemen. Mughīrah ibn Shu'bah (ﷺ) narrated, 'The Messenger of Allah (ﷺ) wore a Roman (Byzantine) *Jubbah* (long shirt) which had narrow sleeves.'

This shows that he was not attached to any particular region or fabric but preferred garments that were modest and comfortable.

- **Sandals/Slippers:** The Prophet (ﷺ) wore simple **sandals with two straps**, made of leather. Anas ibn Mālik (ﷺ) described the Prophet's (ﷺ) sandals in detail, saying, "*The sandals of the Prophet had two straps.*" (Reported by Bukhārī).

Despite receiving gifts of luxurious footwear, the Prophet (ﷺ) preferred these simple sandals, as he always preferred simple and practical items over anything extravagant.

- **Gift from Abyssinia:** There is a narration that the King of Abyssinia (Negus) gifted the Prophet (ﷺ) a pair of either black leather sandals or socks, which the Prophet (ﷺ) wore and even performed *wuḍū'* (ablution) while wearing them.

- **Leather Socks:** Buraydah (رضي الله عنه) relates, 'Negus (رضي الله عنه) the king of Abyssinia sent two simple black coloured leather socks as a gift to the Messenger of Allah (ﷺ). The Messenger (ﷺ) wore them, and when he performed *wuḍū'*, he did *masḥ* (passed wet hands) on them.'

The Prophet Muḥammad (ﷺ) had a simple and healthy diet, emphasising moderation and gratitude. His favourite foods and drinks were not luxurious but were rich in nutrients and easily accessible.

- **Dates:** The Prophet (ﷺ) loved dates and would often break his fast with them. Dates were a staple of the Arabian diet, providing energy and nutrients. He said, "*A household that has dates will never go hungry.*" (Reported by Muslim). He would like to combine dates with cucumbers and watermelon.

- **Honey:** The Prophet (ﷺ) enjoyed honey, which he referred to as a cure for many ailments. Honey is also mentioned in the Qur'ān as a healing substance. The Prophet (ﷺ) often used honey as both food and medicine.

- **Barley Bread:** The Prophet (ﷺ) frequently ate barley bread, a simple yet nutritious food. He would sometimes dip it in vinegar or olive oil. This humble meal reflected his simple lifestyle.

- **Meat:** While the Prophet (ﷺ) liked and ate meat, especially lamb, he did so sparingly. He would eat meat during special occasions or when it was offered by others. He emphasised moderation and never overindulged in food.

- **Gourd (Pumpkin):** The Prophet (ﷺ) loved gourd and would eat it whenever it was served to him. Anas (رضي الله عنه) reported that the Prophet (ﷺ) liked gourd and that he once saw him searching through a dish to find pieces of gourd to eat (Reported by Bukhari).

It was known to be among his favourite foods, reflecting his preference for simple and wholesome nourishment.

- ***Sawīq:*** A traditional dish made from ground wheat or barley, often mixed with water or milk, and sometimes sweetened with dates or honey. It was commonly eaten during the time of the Prophet (ﷺ) because it was simple, nutritious, and easy to prepare.

- ***Hays:*** A sweet dish made from a mixture of *dates, butter (or ghee), and flour.* It's a rich and energy-dense treat that was often served on special occasions. The Prophet (ﷺ) prepared *hays* to serve during his wedding feast with Ṣafiyyah (رضي الله عنها).

These dishes were appreciated for their wholesome ingredients, simplicity, and the natural sweetness of dates, which were a staple in the Arabian diet.

- ***Tharīd:*** One of the favourite dishes of the Prophet Muhammad (ﷺ). It consists of *pieces of bread soaked in a meat or vegetable stew.*

The Prophet (ﷺ) praised *tharīd*, saying: "*The superiority of 'Ā'ishah over other women is like the superiority of tharīd over other dishes.*" (Reported by Bukhari)

- **Water:** The Prophet (ﷺ) loved water and would drink it **sitting down** in ***three sips***, pausing between each one. He encouraged this as the best way to drink water, saying it was more refreshing and healthier. He would always say "*Bismillāh*" before drinking and "*al-ḥamdu-lillāh*" afterward.

- **Milk**: The Prophet (ﷺ) enjoyed milk and praised it for its nourishment. He said, "*There is nothing that serves as both food and drink except for milk.*" (Reported by Tirmidhī).

- ***Nabīdh***: The Prophet (ﷺ) also drank *nabīdh*, a sweet drink made by soaking dates or raisins in water. It was a refreshing drink, providing energy and nutrients without fermentation.

The Sunnah Diet

The Prophet (ﷺ) had simple and healthy eating habits, and he always practiced **moderation** in both eating and drinking. He famously said:

"The son of Adam does not fill any vessel worse than his stomach. It is sufficient for the son of Adam to eat a few bites to keep him standing. But if he must eat, then a third for his food, a third for his drink, and a third for air." (Reported by Tirmidhi)

The Prophet's (ﷺ) balanced diet, with its emphasis on simple and wholesome foods like dates, barley, honey, and water, reflected his desire to stay healthy and maintain a strong connection with Allah.

'Ā'ishah (رضي الله عنها) mentions how at times, two-to-three months would pass and the household of the Prophet (ﷺ) would have had been living on just *aswadayn* – dates and water.

The Prophet (ﷺ) ate in moderation, never overindulging in food. He would eat with three fingers, lick his fingers before he wiped them, and encourage others to sit down while eating.

A companion reports, 'I saw the Prophet (ﷺ) eat with three fingers; the thumb, the finger next to it (index finger) and the middle finger. Then I saw him lick the three fingers before he wiped them, first the middle finger, then the index finger and then the thumb.' (Reported by Ṭabarānī)

Jābir (رضي الله عنه) reports, 'The Prophet (ﷺ) commanded that the plate and the fingers should be licked because one does not know where the *barakah* (blessing) lies.' (Reported by Abū Ya'lā)

The Prophet (ﷺ) did not eat on a table till he died, and he did not eat bread baked from fine flour till he died.

He never ever criticised food: if he liked it, he would eat it, otherwise he would leave it.

SOME SUNNAH FOODS & DRINKS

Honey

Black Seed

Gourd

Meat

Dates

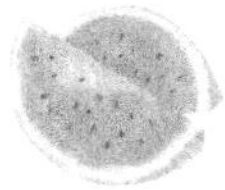

Watermelon

Cucumber

Vinegar

Olives

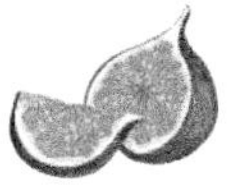

Fig

Beetroot

Bread

Talbīnah
(mixture of barley flour, milk & honey)

Milk

Tharīd
(mixture of bread cooked into the stew)

Hays/Sawīq
(mixture of dates with butter/ghee & flour)

The Prophet Muḥammad (ﷺ) placed great emphasis on cleanliness, considering it an essential part of faith. His daily hygiene practices reflect his attention to personal care and his teachings about purity.

- ***Siwāk*** **(Toothstick):** The Prophet (ﷺ) regularly used a *siwāk*, a natural toothstick, to clean his teeth, and he also used it on his tongue. Ibn 'Abbās (رضي الله عنهما) reported that the Prophet (ﷺ) used the *siwāk* so frequently that his Companions thought a verse regarding it would be revealed. He encouraged its use, saying, "*If it weren't difficult for my ummah (community), I would have commanded them to use the siwāk before every prayer.*"

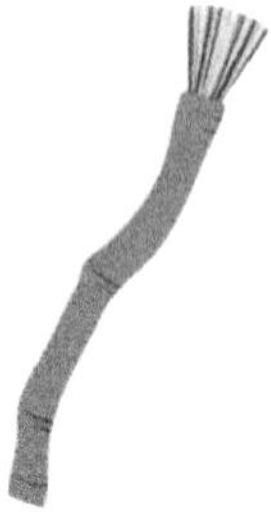

- **Oiling and Combing Hair:** The Prophet (ﷺ) frequently oiled and combed his hair and beard, commencing from the right side, keeping them neat and clean.

Anas (رضي الله عنه) reported that the Prophet's (ﷺ) hair reached his shoulders and was always well-groomed.

- ***Koḥl*** **(Collyrium – e.g. Antimony Sulphide):** The Prophet (ﷺ) applied *koḥl* to his eyes, made from *ithmid*, which helps to strengthen the eyesight and promote the growth of eyelashes. Ibn 'Abbās (رضي الله عنهما) reported that the Prophet (ﷺ) applied *koḥl* to his eyes three times every night.

The Prophet Muḥammad (ﷺ) was known for his exemplary character, which attracted people to him and made even his harshest enemies soften toward him.

- **Kindness:** The Prophet (ﷺ) was always gentle and compassionate toward others. Whether it was children, the elderly, or strangers, he treated everyone with respect and care. He said, "*The best of you are those who are kindest to their families.*" (Reported by Tirmidhī)

- **Generosity:** The Prophet (ﷺ) was known for his unmatched generosity. Even when he had little, he gave freely to others. He once said, "*The best of people are those who bring the most benefit to others.*"

- **Forgiveness:** Despite the harsh treatment he received from his enemies, the Prophet (ﷺ) always forgave them. During the conquest of Makkah, he forgave the very people who had driven him out of his home and persecuted his followers, saying, "*Go, for you are free.*"

- **Humility:** Despite his status as a Prophet and leader, the Prophet (ﷺ) was incredibly humble. He performed household chores, mended his own clothes, and never sought special treatment. Anas ibn Mālik (رضي الله عنه), who served the Prophet (ﷺ) for ten years, said, "He never said to me, '*Why did you do this?*' or '*Why did you not do that?*'" (Reported by Bukhārī)

- **Patience:** The Prophet (ﷺ) exhibited remarkable patience, whether in the face of personal hardships, insults, or challenges to his mission. He never allowed anger to control his actions, always responding with calmness and wisdom.

بَلَغَ العُلَى بِكَـــــمَالِه كَشَفَ الدُّجَى بِجَمَالِه
حَسُنَــتْ جَمِيعُ خِصَالِه صَلُّوا عَلَـــــيْهِ وَآلِه

He reached the heights with his elegance,
He lit up darknesses with his achievements,
He beautified every one of his good qualities,
So, send salutations upon him and his family.

HOW THE PROPHET (ﷺ) TREATED OTHERS

One of the most remarkable aspects of the Prophet Muhammad's (ﷺ) life was how he treated people, regardless of their background, age, or status. He had a special way of making everyone feel valued, important, and respected.

His Family

The Prophet (ﷺ) was a loving father, husband, and grandfather. His kindness and compassion were especially noticeable in how he treated his family.

- **Towards His Wives:** The Prophet (ﷺ) was known to be gentle and caring with his wives. He would help with household chores and never showed any signs of arrogance. His wife 'Ā'ishah (رضي الله عنها) once said that he would fix his own shoes, sew his clothes, and help in the house, even though he was a leader.

- **Towards His Children:** The Prophet (ﷺ) loved his children deeply and he loved to play with children in general. He would often carry his grandchildren, play with them, and show them affection.

When his daughter, Fāṭimah (رضي الله عنها), would visit him, he would stand up, kiss her, and offer her his seat. This was unusual in a society where daughters were often treated with less care than sons, but the Prophet (ﷺ) showed through his actions that all children deserve love and respect.

- **Towards His Grandchildren:** His love for his grandchildren, Ḥasan and Ḥusayn (رضي الله عنهما), was well-known. He would carry them on his shoulders and play with them in the streets. Even while giving sermons in the mosque, if they came to him, he would pick them up and continue his speech while holding them.

Anas (رضي الله عنه) reported that the Prophet (ﷺ) would often play with his granddaughter

Zaynab and call her affectionately by the nickname, "*O Zuwaynib.*"

His Friends and Companions

The Prophet (ﷺ) was a true friend to his Companions. He listened to them, advised them, and cared for their well-being. He never made anyone feel unimportant or ignored.

- **Equality:** He treated all his companions equally, whether they were rich or poor, strong or weak. If he was sitting with his Companions, it was hard to tell who the leader was because he sat and ate just like everyone else.

One time, a man came to meet the Prophet (ﷺ) and was so nervous that he started shaking. The Prophet (ﷺ) smiled and said, "*Relax, I am just the son of a woman who ate simple food.*"

- **Forgiveness and Mercy:** The Prophet (ﷺ) forgave people who wronged him. A famous example is when he returned to Makkah after years of being driven out by the Quraysh, who had fought against him and his followers.

Instead of seeking revenge, the Prophet (ﷺ) forgave them and told them they were free to go. His mercy softened the hearts of even his greatest enemies, leading many of them to accept Islam.

His Treatment of Strangers and the Poor

The Prophet (ﷺ) treated strangers with kindness and always helped those in need, no matter who they were. He showed the same respect and love to the poor and to orphans as he did to everyone else.

- **Helping the Needy:** The Prophet (ﷺ) was known for his generosity. He would never turn away anyone who came to him for help, even if he had very little to give. He would often give away all his food, money, and clothes to those who needed them more. He once said, *"The best of you are those who feed others and greet those you know and those you do not know."*

- **Respecting the Elderly and Children:** The Prophet (ﷺ) always showed respect to the elderly and taught his followers to do the same. He said, "*He is not one of us who does not show mercy to our young and respect for our elders.*"

He also showed great affection to children and loved to play with them. He taught people that children should be treated with love and never ignored.

The daily life of the Prophet Muhammad (ﷺ) was simple but full of wisdom. He lived a life of balance, making sure to take care of his responsibilities while also spending time in worship, reflection, and caring for others. Learning about his daily habits can inspire us to follow a balanced, healthy, and spiritually fulfilling life.

Morning Routine

The Prophet (ﷺ) would begin his day by waking up early, well before dawn. His first action was to praise and thank Allah. Then he would make ablution and perform ***Tahajjud*** (the night prayer), which he loved and encouraged his companions to perform. He would conclude this with his ***witr*** prayer as he approached dawn.

Before ***Fajr*** (the early morning prayer), he would use the ***siwāk*** (a natural toothbrush) to clean his teeth, showing the importance of hygiene.

Upon performing the two units of ***sunnah* prayers** of the *fajr* prayer, he would **lie down directly on the ground** for a brief period before making his way to lead the *fajr* prayer.

After the *Fajr* prayer, the Prophet (ﷺ) would often sit in the mosque, engaging in quiet reflection and ***dhikr*** (remembrance of Allah), and at times would address his Companions.

Work and Community Engagement

After the *fajr* prayer, the Prophet (ﷺ) would engage in his daily tasks, whether that involved attending to his family, visiting the sick, resolving disputes, or teaching his companions. He believed in being productive and staying active.

- **Helping Others:** Throughout the day, the Prophet (ﷺ) would be available to help those in need, answer questions, and offer advice. If someone asked for his help, he would never refuse. He said, *"The best of people are those who bring the most benefit to others."*

- **Time for Rest:** In the middle of the day, the Prophet (ﷺ) would take a short nap, called a ***qaylūlah*** (siesta), to refresh himself. He encouraged others to rest as well, saying that this small nap would help people stay energetic for the rest of the day.

Evening Routine

In the evening, the Prophet (ﷺ) would wind down with time for reflection and prayer.

He would perform the ***'Isha*** prayer (night prayer) and encourage others to complete their responsibilities before going to bed.

- **Bedtime Rituals:** Before sleeping, the Prophet (ﷺ) would recite verses from the Qur'ān, including the ***Āyat al-Kursīy***, ***Sūrah al-Ikhlāṣ***, ***Sūrah al-Falaq***, and ***Sūrah An-Nās***.

He would blow into his hands and wipe them over his body for protection.

He would also recite the **last two verses of *Sūrah al-Baqarah*.**

Jābir (RA) narrates, the Messenger (ﷺ) would not sleep until he had recited the

Tanzīl (***Sūrah as-Sajdah***) and *Tabārak* (***Sūrah al-Mulk***).

He would also sleep on his right side and say a short prayer before closing his eyes.

- **Gratitude:** The Prophet (ﷺ) taught his companions the importance of ending the day with gratitude to Allah, thanking Him for the blessings of the day and asking for protection during the night.

HOW CAN WE FOLLOW THE PROPHET'S (ﷺ) EXAMPLE?

The life of the Prophet Muḥammad (ﷺ) is the perfect guide for us in every aspect of life. His habits, his kindness, his humility, and his love for others should inspire us to follow his example. By learning about him and striving to embody his characteristics, we can draw closer to Allah and become better individuals.

Here are some practical ways we can follow his example:

1. **Kindness:** Treat everyone with kindness and compassion, regardless of their background, just as the Prophet (ﷺ) did.

2. **Generosity**: Be generous with your time, your wealth, and your kindness. Help others whenever you can, as the Prophet (ﷺ) helped those in need.

3. **Gratitude:** Always be thankful to Allah for every blessing, no matter how small, and

express that gratitude in your prayers and actions.

4. **Simplicity:** Live a life of modesty and simplicity, focusing on what truly matters—your relationship with Allah and your treatment of others.

5. **Forgiveness:** Forgive those who wrong you, just as the Prophet (ﷺ) forgave even his worst enemies. Let go of anger and resentment, and show mercy to others.

By incorporating these qualities into our daily lives, we can follow the example of our beloved Prophet (ﷺ) and achieve success in this world and the hereafter.

May Allah guide us all to follow in the footsteps of His Messenger (ﷺ).

CONNECTING WITH THE BELOVED PROPHET (ﷺ)

In striving to strengthen our spiritual connection with the beloved Prophet Muhammad (ﷺ), the path is clear: we must seek to emulate him in every aspect of our lives.

1. **By adopting his *Sunnah***—his habits, practices, and way of life—we can bring the light of his example into our daily routines.

2. **His noble *akhlāq* (character)** was a manifestation of perfection—kindness, humility, patience, and sincerity. As we personify these traits, we draw nearer to the divine love that the Prophet (ﷺ) radiated.

- Both of these can only be truly attained by studying and connecting with both his ***Sīrah*** and his ***Shamā'il***.
- We have provided a few examples of both *Sīrah* and *Shamā'il* on pages 52-53.

3. Additionally, through consistent and heartfelt *ṣalawāt/durūd* (**salutations of peace and blessings**) upon him, we keep his presence alive in our hearts and nurture our love for him.

4. This love also calls us to **adopt his mission** as our own—to feel the ***pain and concern*** for the well-being and success of **his *Ummah***, and to work toward their success in both this world and the hereafter.

Let us make his mission our mission, serving Allah and caring for humanity as he did, so that we may be worthy of standing in his company and drinking from his blessed hands on the Day of Judgment, by Allah's grace.

BOOKS ON THE SHAMĀ'IL

Take your study of the blessed *Shamā'il* further through the following recommendations:

The Khulāṣa

Shaykh M. A.H. al-Kattānī

[Turath Publishing]

Khaṣā'il

[Shamā'il of Imām Tirmidhī]

Shaykh M Zakariyyā Kāndhlawī

[Turath Publishing]

Shama'il

Study Book

[Abu Zahra Press]

Al-Shamā'il

Al-Muḥammadiyyah

Imām M. I. Al-Tirmidhī

BOOKS ON THE SĪRAH

Keep reading further on the life of our Beloved (ﷺ) through the following recommendations:

Muḥammad ﷺ

Sayyid A.H. 'Alī Nadwī

[UK Islamic Academy]

Seeratul Mustafa

[Abridged]

Shaykh M. Idrīs Kāndhlawī

[Zam Zam Publishing]

The Sealed Nectar

Saifur-Rahman Mubarakpuri

[Darussalam]

Sīratul Muṣṭafā [3 v.]

Shaykh M. Idrīs Kāndhlawī

[Zam Zam Publishers]

Information About the Beloved Messenger (ﷺ)

Name and Genealogy:

Muḥammad (ﷺ)
ibn (son of) 'Abdullāh
ibn 'Abd al-Muṭṭalib
ibn Hāshim
ibn 'Abd Manāf
ibn Quṣayy
ibn Kilāb
ibn Murrah
ibn Ka'b
ibn Lu'ayy
ibn Ghālib
ibn Fihr
ibn Mālik
ibn an-Naḍr
ibn Kinānah
ibn Khuzaymah
ibn Mudrikah
ibn Ilyās
ibn Muḍr
ibn Nizār
ibn Ma'd
ibn 'Adnān [from the progeny of Ismā'īl (عليه السلام) *ibn* Ibrāhīm (عليه السلام)]

Mother's Genealogy

Āminah
bint (daughter of) Wahab
ibn 'Abd Munāf
ibn Zuhrah
ibn Kilāb – [here the lineage of his parents join]

Date of Birth: Monday 8th/9th (according to some narrations 12th) Rabī' al-Awwal, known as the year of the Elephant, corresponding with the Gregorian date, 20th/22nd of April 571 C.E.

Date of Demise: Monday, 12th Rabī' al-Awwal, 11th year of Hijrah; aged 63 years and 4 days.

Names of the Prophet's (ﷺ) wives

1. Khadījah رضي الله عنها *bint* Khuwaylid
2. Sawdah رضي الله عنها *bint* Zam'ah
3. 'Ā'ishah رضي الله عنها *bint* Abī Bakr رضي الله عنه
4. Ḥafṣah رضي الله عنها *bint* 'Umar *ibn* al-Khaṭṭāb رضي الله عنه
5. Zaynab رضي الله عنها *bint* Khuzaymah
6. Umm Salamah, Hind رضي الله عنها *bint* Abī Umayyah
7. Zaynab رضي الله عنها *bint* Jaḥash
8. Juwayriyyah رضي الله عنها *bint* al-Ḥārith
9. Umm Ḥabībah, Ramlah رضي الله عنها *bint* Abī Sufyān رضي الله عنه

10. Ṣafiyyah ﵂ *bint* Ḥuyayy *ibn* Akhtab
11. Maymūnah ﵂ bint al-Ḥārith

Bondswomen of the Prophet (ﷺ)

1. Māriyah Qibṭiyyah ﵂ - *the mother of the Prophet's son Ibrāhīm* ﵁
2. Rayḥānah ﵂ *bint* Sham'ūn
3. Nafīsah ﵂

Children of the Prophet (ﷺ)

Daughters:

1. Zaynab ﵂
2. Ruqayyah ﵂
3. Umm Kulthūm ﵂
4. Fāṭimah ﵂

Sons:

1. Qāsim ﵁
2. 'Abdullāh ﵁
3. Ibrāhīm ﵁

All of the Prophet's (ﷺ) children were born through his marriage with Khadījah ﵂

except for his son Ibrāhīm ﷺ, whose mother was the Prophet's bondswoman Māriyah ﷺ.

The Various Names of the Prophet (ﷺ)

Various names for the Messenger (ﷺ) have also been mentioned in the Qur'ān, and he also referred to himself by multiple names and titles which have been recorded in the collections of *aḥādīth*.

Similarly, the 'Ulamā' have collated hundreds of countless names and titles of the Beloved Messenger (ﷺ) over the course of history.

Those mentioned in the Qur'ān are:

1. Muḥammad (the praised)
2. Aḥmad (the most praising)
3. Shāhid (the witness)
4. Mubash-shir (the giver of glad tidings)
5. Nadhīr (the fore-warner)
6. Mubīn (the clear proof/evident)
7. Dā'ī ila-llāh (the caller to Allah)
8. as-Sirāj al-Munīr (the bright lamp),
9. Mudhakkir (the reminder),

10. Raḥmat li-l-'Ālamīn (the mercy for the worlds),
11. Ni'mah (the blessing),
12. Shahīd (the witness/witnessed),
13. al-Amīn (the trustworthy),
14. al-Muzzammil (the one wrapped in garment)
15. al-Muddath-thir (the one enveloped in garment)

Those mentioned in the authentic Ḥadīth collections are:

1. Muḥammad (the praised)
2. Aḥmad (the most praised)
3. Māḥī (the eraser - *of falsehood*)
4. Ḥāshir (the gatherer – *on the Day of Judgement*)
5. 'Āqib (the last of Prophets)
6. Qāsim (the distributor)
7. Nabiyy ar-Raḥmah (the Prophet of mercy)
8. Nabiyy at-Tawbah (the Prophet of repentance)
9. Muqaffī (follower of other Prophets)
10. Abū al-Qāsim (father of Qāsim)

Printed in Dunstable, United Kingdom

67438293R00037